BOOK ANALYSIS

Written by Claire Cornillon
Translated by Soline de Dorlodot

AF143896

The Idiot

BY FYODOR DOSTOYEVSKY

Bright
≡**Summaries**.com

FYODOR DOSTOYEVSKY

RUSSIAN AUTHOR

- **Born in Moscow in 1821**
- **Died in St Petersburg in 1881**
- **Notable works:**
  - *Crime and Punishment* (1866), novel
  - *The Idiot* (1868), novel
  - *The Brothers Karamazov* (1880), novel

Fyodor Dostoyevsky was born in Moscow in 1821. Considered one of the greatest Russian writers, he is remembered for his metaphysical reflections and patriotic commitment.

His most famous works were published in Europe during his exile due to his acquaintance with a group of Russian progressionists. Thus, *Crime and Punishment* (1866) and *The Idiot* (1868) marked the beginning of the author's maturity phase. Dostoyevsky was met with acclaim upon his return to Russia in 1871. His last novel, *The Brothers Karamazov* (1880), was published a few months before his death in St Petersburg in 1881.

THE IDIOT

A NOVEL WITH MANY TWISTS

- **Genre:** novel
- **Reference edition:** Dostoyevsky, F. (2008) *The Idiot*. Trans. Martin, E. Kansas: Digireads.com Publishing.
- **First edition:** 1869
- **Themes:** love, goodness, social climbing, ethics, social classes, free will

The Idiot, published in 1869, is a long novel with a complex narration and structure, which tells the story of Prince Myshkin, a good and naïve man who suffers from epilepsy and whom the other people often call an idiot. Back in Russia after a long stay in Switzerland, he befriends a series of characters. He loves Nastassya Filippovna who humiliated and rejected him, but has also feelings for Aglaya Epanchina. Towards the end of the novel, the Prince is driven back to his illness, after the murder of Nastassya. The many twists and the tensions between the various characters are excuses for the author to ask wider questions about God, evil and free will.

SUMMARY

Lebedyev, Rogozhin and the Prince Nikolayevich Myshkin, who has spent his youth in Switzerland to cure his epileptic fits and is now back in Russia, meet in a third-class carriage. Once in St Petersburg, the Prince visits the wife of the General Epanchin. She also belongs to the Myshkin family, but she is a distant relative and he would like to get to know her. The general welcomes him distrustfully, but finally invites him in. This is how the Prince integrates into the circle of the Epanchins' friends.

Afanasy Ivanovich Totsky, a man of about fifty years, would like to marry one of the daughters of the General Epanchin. However, he had taken in an orphaned young girl when she was young, Nastassya Filippovna, and now that she has become an adult, her character has entirely changed and he says that she conspires to prevent his happiness. Frightened by Nastassya, he fears that she will stand in the way of his marriage. He goes to see her with the general: the matter seems to be resolved, but Afanasy remains anxious.

The Prince is introduced to the wife of the general and their daughters, Alexandra, Adelaida and Aglaya. They start a conversation about his genealogy, his history, his illness – he had epilepsy: "His fits were so frequent then, that they made almost an idiot of him (the Prince used the expression 'idiot' himself)"– then about art and life. The Prince wishes to go to Nastassya Filippovna, as Rogozhin, who is in love with her, mentioned her during their train ride. He wants to warn her that she should not marry Gavrila Ardalionovich, because he only wants her for her money. Rogozhin arrives, drunk, with a hundred thousand rubles to pay for one night with Nastassya. Nastassya condemns the greed of men. The Prince falls in love with Nastassya and offers to marry her, but she humiliates and rejects him, and elopes with Rogozhin.

PART II

The Prince inherits money from one of his aunts and leaves for Moscow for six months, to get his affairs in order. Myshkin tries to convince Rogozhin not to marry Nastassya. Rogozhin, understanding that Myshkin is a rival, tries to murder him, but the Prince suffers an epileptic fit and Rogozhin flees. Myshkin is put up by Lebedyev during his recovery.

Later, an article accuses Myshkin of refusing to give Mr. Burdovsky his part of the inheritance, the latter presumably being the son of Pavlishchev. However, the Prince provides an explanation and shows that he is a fraud: Burdovsky has been manipulated and is not the son of Pavlishchev.

PART 3

Lizaveta Prokofyevna, the general's wife, thinks about the marriage of her three daughters. There is a rumor that the Prince is in a relationship with Aglaya, which upsets Lizaveta. However, despite the love the Prince has for Aglaya, nothing happened between them. Moreover, the Prince corrects the young woman by telling her that he has no intention of asking for her hand in marriage. Then, an incident involving Nastassya Filippovna happens and ends brutally. The love triangle between the two women and the Prince becomes conflictual.

Another incident happens during the Prince's birthday: a young man suffering from tuberculosis, Ippolit, reads a document in which he explains why he is going to commit suicide and then tries to shoot himself in the head. However, he fails to do so because he had forgotten to load the gun.

Nastassya sends letters to Aglaya, in which her feelings for the Prince transpire. She writes: "Do you know, I think you ought to love me – for you are the same in my eyes as in his – you are as light. An angel cannot hate, perhaps cannot love, either." She goes to meet Myshkin and asks him if he is happy. Rogozhin brings her back with him and the Prince tells her that he is not happy.

PART 4

The relationship between Aglaya and the Prince is very ambiguous. She loves him, but publicly rejects him, because she cannot accept his strangeness. During a party they throw, the Epanchins would like to introduce the Prince to the world. The latter launches into a passionate speech about religion and, because of a clumsy movement, breaks a vase. Then, he tries to resume his speech, but he has an epileptic fit and collapses.

When the Prince has recovered, Aglaya asks Nastassya and Rogozhin to come to have a frank discussion; she accuses Nastassya of having tormented the Prince, of having rejected him and of trying to hinder their relationship. The Prince tries to calm Aglaya's violence by defending Nastassya. Aglaya cannot bear it and flees. The Prince starts running after her and seeing this, Nastassya loses consciousness: thus, the Prince stays by her side.

The Prince confesses that Nastassya frightens him, but that he loves her and also has feelings for Aglaya. The Prince and Nastassya decide to marry, but on the day of the wedding, she elopes with Rogozhin. The Prince starts looking for her and finds Rogozhin next to the body of Nastassya, whom he has murdered. He is arrested. As for Aglaya, she marries against her family's will a man she believes to be a Polish Count and who turns out to be a fraud.

CHARACTER STUDY

PRINCE MYSHKIN

Prince Lev Nikolayevich Myshkin is a 26-year-old young man who suffers from epilepsy and was nursed in Switzerland. At the beginning of the novel, he comes back to Russia, his home country, to integrate into the society of St Petersburg.

First and foremost, he is a mysterious character. All the other characters wonder about him throughout the story and do not know how to interpret his behavior, because he acts in a surprising manner, independently from the social norms. Thus, he seems very naïve and sincere when he talks with the other characters. He is defined by his illness and his innocence, which results in other people often calling him an idiot. However, he is clear-sighted where psychology is concerned, he is knowledgeable and has a very well-thought-out perspective on life.

It is also thanks to his goodness that he manages to be accepted by the people he meets. Thus, when he is introduced to the general, the latter first perceives him with distrust, but is soon charmed: "The Prince's expression was so good-natured at this moment, and so entirely free from even a suspicion of unpleasant feeling was the smile with which he looked at the general as he spoke, that the latter suddenly paused, and appeared to gaze at his guest from quite a new point of view, all in an instant."

He also embodies gentleness and compassion. He takes care

of Nastassya when she loses consciousness and stays with Rogozhin, even though the latter has become mad after having killed Nastassya.

Therefore, because of his sincerity and goodness, he is the most vulnerable to the world of lies and plots he lives in. Aglaya says that she never met someone that could equal him in the noble simplicity of his soul and his loving, boundless trust. However, although he is a deeply good and loving man, he only manages to create more violence and happiness around him.

He loses Aglaya and Nastassya dies. This failure is crystallized in the resumption of his epileptic fits at the end of the novel, as if the troubles around him had finally gotten to him.

NASTASSYA AND ROGOZHIN

Nastassya Filippovna and Parfyon Semyonovich Rogozhin are a parallel couple to the one formed by the Prince and Aglaya, thus creating not a triangle, but a tragic love quartet.

Rogozhin, the son of a merchant, is a sort of double of the Prince, but a violent double. He tries to kill him and finally murders Nastassya. Throughout the novel, Nastassya keeps eloping with him out of spite, and does not truly love him. This rivalry with the Prince leads Rogozhin to commit the murder.

Nastassya is a proud and scandalous woman, who constantly tries to prove that she is though. She is unhappy and has a bad self-perception, which prevents her from accepting the Prince's love, as she feels unworthy. However, she also denounces the stupidity that surrounds her, and her behavior betrays her suffering. She exclaims: "I had better go on to the streets, or accept Rogozhin, or become a washerwoman or something—for I have nothing of my own, you know. I shall go away and leave everything behind, to the last rag—he shall have it all back. And who would take me without anything?" (Part I Chapter 15). Moreover, she truly loves the Prince. Consequently, she is an ambiguous character, both fascinating and frightening.

THE EPANCHIN FAMILY

The Epanchin family welcomes the Prince into their midst. It is made up of the General, his wife, Lisaveta, who is also a Myshkin, like the Prince, and their three daughters, Alexandra, Adelaida and Aglaya. None of them are married, a situation which their mother is trying to remedy.

Aglaya turns out to be a very important character because the Prince falls in love with her. But she adopts an ambiguous attitude towards him. Aware of his love for Nastassya, she often mocks him. Yet her position is much clearer than that of Nastassya: she is the one who finally arranges for the actors of this sad quartet to meet and during that conversation, she is the most honest of all, so that she finally breaks, because her sincerity presents the Prince with an ultimatum: Nastassya or her. Even though Aglaya somehow represents high society, the love that the Prince bears for her is less absolute than that which he feels for Nastassya. Aglaya is careful of her image; this explains her behavior towards the Prince.

ANALYSIS

A COMPLEX STORY

The novel tells a complex story with several layers.

First of all, Dostoyevsky builds a narration in which characters are abound, and whose stories or nature the narrator sometimes explains, thus creating digressions within the novel, making it more complicated. Thus, Part 4 begins with a portrait of Varvara Ardalionovna, her husband Mr. Ptitisyn and her brother Gavrila Ardalionovich. Moreover, the characters themselves sometimes turn into narrators in dialogues and tell stories or memories that enrich the narration. For example, this is the case of Prince Myshkin when he meets the General's wife and daughters and tells them stories about his past.

Consequently, many plots appear, which upset the lives of the characters: lies, violence and conflicts are everywhere in the four parts of the novel. Rumor also has a very important place, with everybody trying to guess what the others are doing. Everything happens in a corrupted society where money is the first motor of action for the characters.

It is in that context that the main intrigue is built, which is also complicated in itself: the doomed love story between the Prince and Nastassya on one side, the Prince and Aglaya on another side, and finally, Nastassya and Rogozhin. In this quartet, everybody ends up being unhappy. They inflict sufferings upon each other, sometimes on purpose and sometimes involuntarily.

The love of the Prince for Nastassya is especially ambiguous, because he says that he is frightened of her face, yet loves her: in this, Nastassya represents the sublime, that which is both fascinating and terrifying. The love that the Prince bears for her is a love of the absolute and can be compared to the notion of transcendence. As for Aglaya, she belongs to the society of men, but she is also ambiguous because she torments the Prince by treating him the way she does in public. The Prince's plot finally takes a turn for the worst. His goodness is crushed by the weight of the lies and vices that are dominant in the society in which he lives.

Then, the love story between the different characters raises social and political questions about Russia, and mostly offers a metaphysical interpretation, an interrogation about Man, which makes the novel even more complex.

ETHICS

The sentimental intrigue in the novel is the basis for a reflection about Man, in that the great number of characters and the ties that are being woven between them form an especially complex view of Man's relation to life. Not only does the narrator himself open some chapters or parts with a theoretical explanation about an aspect of existence which he then links to one or several characters of his story, but some of the characters themselves talk with more or less enthusiasm about various topics, such as art, the meaning of life or politics, usually at parties or social events. The sum of these speeches draws the lines of several underlying problematics.

Thus, the novel asks questions about the notion of good and sincerity. The Prince embodies these notions, yet unhappiness follows him. The other characters keep lying, spreading false rumors, as in the episode of the Prince's inheritance, and play a social role. At Nastassya's, when the guests are asked to tell the worst thing they ever did, the aim is not to be sincere, but to establish power relations between them depending on how they behave regarding the game. However, the Prince thinks constantly in terms of morality and tries to act in a good way and to be sincere, really expecting a punishment. It is precisely because the Prince does not play the social game of power and pride that he always seems strange to the other characters.

The plots and twists also convey a reflection about the relation of the individual person to the group. The narrator disserts among other things about the matter of originality. The Prince is indeed an original being, because he stands out by refusing to join the social game, but the other characters are looking for another sort of originality, a form of social success: the aim is to outshine the other members of the group. As highlighted by the narrator, some people are ready to anything, even to commit a crime, to stand out. Thus, the narrator says about Gavrila that: "A deep and unchangeable consciousness of his own lack of talent, combined with a vast longing to be able to persuade himself that he was original, had rankled in his heart, even from childhood."

For example, the novel also examines the matter of the meaning of life. Ippolit's speech illustrates the question of free will. He, who is going to die in a few weeks, wonders if suicide is the only way to keep control over his life.: "And finally, nature has so limited my capacity for work or activity of any kind, in allotting me but three weeks of time, that suicide is about the only thing left that I can begin and end in the time of my own free will. Perhaps then I am anxious to take advantage of my last chance of doing something for myself. A protest is sometimes no small thing." Earlier in the novel, the Prince also wonders about life and man's ability to act: "And then it struck me that life may be grand enough even in a prison". The question of action is not only a material question, it is also a matter of willpower and decision, so that even enclosed between four walls, the spirit of a man can be free.

THE RECURRENCE OF RELIGIOUS MOTIVES

The novel is also structured around metaphysical and religious questions. The figure of Christ is namely recurrent throughout the pictorial motives about which the characters talk. Indeed, Dostoyevsky was struck by *The Body of the Dead Christ in the Tomb* by Holbein (German painter, 1498-1543), a painting representing the Christ in his tomb with the realism of an actual body, which raised the question of faith with the writer: with Christ so marked by death, how can one believe in his upcoming resurrection? Several characters of the novel talk about this work, echoing the author's thoughts.

Some discussions are about religion and specifically about Christianity. The Prince's stance on religion is very interesting. He violently attacks Catholicism, precisely because of the way it depicts good and suffering: "Atheism only preaches a negation, but Romanism goes further; it preaches a disfigured, distorted Christ". He accuses it of being a road towards atheism, which he rejects above all else. He says to Rogozhin: "The essence of religious feeling has nothing to do with reason, or atheism, or crime, or acts of any kind—it has nothing to do with these things—and never had. There is something besides all this, something which the arguments of the atheists can never touch." In fact, the problem of faith is tackled throughout the novel. That which matters for Dostoyevsky is not so much reason as "this religious feeling", namely the inner experience, belonging to that which cannot be said.

The Prince talks about his epileptic fits in religious terms, as if they were mystical crises, and as if his illness gave him access to the world: "This would continue for three or four days, and then I would recover myself again. I remember my melancholy was intolerable; I felt inclined to cry; I sat and wondered and wondered uncomfortably; the consciousness that everything was strange weighed terribly upon me; I could understand that it was all foreign and strange". Furthermore:

> "What matter though it be only disease, an abnormal tension of the brain, if when I recall and analyze the moment, it seems to have been one of harmony and beauty in the highest degree—an instant of deepest sensation, overflowing with unbounded joy and rapture, ecstatic devotion, and completest life?"

Consequently, the character has sometimes been likened to a Christ-like figure, a compassionate being that becomes the representative of the sufferings of Men. However, this character should not be reduced to this interpretation.

FURTHER REFLECTION

SOME QUESTIONS TO THINK ABOUT...

- Why is the Prince called an idiot? In your opinion, is this true?
- What is the place of the narrator in the story? How does he act within the story?
- How does the novel depict the bourgeois society of St Petersburg?
- Compare Nastassya and Aglaya.
- What role does Rogozhin play in the plot?
- Take note of the various comments about the representation of Christ. What are the preeminent themes in these various extracts?
- What kind of relationship to life does Myshkin embody?
- Compare the attitude of the Prince at the beginning and the end of the novel: what has changed? How would you describe the plot he follows throughout the novel?

We want to hear from you!
Leave a comment on your online library
and share your favourite books on social media!

FURTHER READING

REFERENCE EDITION

- Dostoyevsky, F. (2008) *The Idiot*. Trans. Martin, E. Kansas: Digireads.com Publishing.

MORE FROM BRIGHTSUMMARIES.COM

- Reading guide – *Crime and Punishment* by Fyodor Dostoyevsky